KIDS ON EARTH

Wildlife Adventures – Explore The World

Mahi Mahi - Costa Rica

Sensei Paul David

COPYRIGHT PAGE

www.senseipublishing.com

@senseipublishing
#senseipublishing

Synopsis

This book provides an introduction to the Mahi Mahi, a popular fish found in the waters of Costa Rica. It explores 30 fun facts about the Mahi Mahi, including its unique color pattern, its migratory habits, and its importance to the ocean's food web. It also covers the Mahi Mahi's role in commercial and recreational fisheries, its sensitivity to changes in its environment, and its importance as a source of food for humans. Finally, the book concludes with a synopsis that highlights the Mahi Mahi's importance to Costa Rica's culture and its resilience in adapting to changing conditions in its habitat.

Get Our FREE Books Now!

kidsonearth.life

kidsonearth.world

Click Below for Another Book In Each Series

senseipublishing.com/KoE_SERIES

senseipublishing.com/KoE_Wildlife_SERIES

KoE En Español

senseipublishing.com/KoE_SERIES_SPANISH

Join Our Publishing Journey!

If you would like to receive FUTURE FREE BOOKS and get to know us better, please click www.senseipublishing.com and join our newsletter by entering your email address in the pop-up box.

Follow Our Blog: senseipauldavid.ca

Follow/Like/Subscribe: Facebook, Instagram, YouTube: @senseipublishing

Scan the QR Code with your phone or tablet to follow us on social media:

Like / Subscribe / Follow

Introduction

Welcome to the wonderful world of the Mahi Mahi, an amazing fish that can be found in the waters of Costa Rica. This book will take you through 30 fun facts about the Mahi Mahi that will help you to learn more about them, their habits, and their environment. So, without further ado, let's dive in!

The Mahi Mahi is one of the most popularly eaten fish in Costa Rica. It's a great source of protein, full of vitamins and minerals, and has a mild, sweet flavor.

3

The Mahi Mahi is a very strong swimmer and is able to reach speeds of up to 50 mph!

The Mahi Mahi has a unique color pattern, consisting of yellow, green, and blue stripes that are visible when the fish is in the water.

Mahi Mahi can live up to five years in the wild.

Mahi Mahi can be found in the waters of Costa Rica, as well as other countries in Central and South America.

11

The Mahi Mahi is an important food source for many people in Costa Rica and is often served in restaurants.

13

The Mahi Mahi is a popular game fish and is often caught by sport fishermen.

15

Mahi Mahi mate for life, and each pair will establish a territory that they will defend against intruders.

17

The Mahi Mahi is a fast-growing fish, reaching sexual maturity at just a year old.

The Mahi Mahi has a very short spawning season, lasting only a few weeks each year.

The Mahi Mahi is an important part of the ocean's food web, as it is a prey fish for many larger predators.

23

The Mahi Mahi is a highly migratory species and can travel thousands of miles in search of food.

Mahi Mahi are sensitive to changes in their environment and can be used as an indicator of the health of the ocean.

The Mahi Mahi can be found in shallow waters near the shore, as well as in deeper parts of the ocean.

Mahi Mahi can grow up to three feet in length and can weigh up to 20 pounds.

31

The Mahi Mahi has an average lifespan of four to five years.

The Mahi Mahi is a carnivore that feeds on small fish, crustaceans, and squid.

The Mahi Mahi is an important species for commercial fisheries, and its meat is highly sought after.

37

Mahi Mahi are often caught using longline fishing, which can be damaging to the environment and other species.

The Mahi Mahi is an important species for recreational fishing, and is often targeted by anglers.

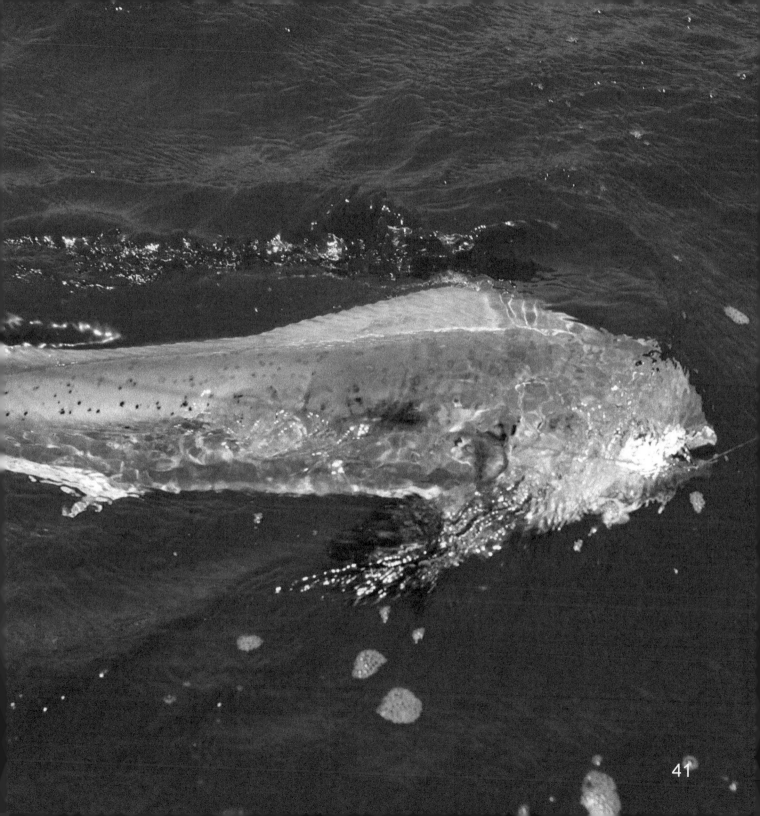

41

The Mahi Mahi is a top predator in its ecosystem, and plays an important role in controlling the populations of its prey.

43

The Mahi Mahi has a high reproductive rate and can produce up to two million eggs per spawn.

Mahi Mahi are highly sensitive to changes in their environment and can be affected by pollution and overfishing.

The Mahi Mahi is a popular fish for aquaculture and is often raised in fish farms.

49

The Mahi Mahi is a great source of food for humans, and its meat is high in nutrients.

51

The Mahi Mahi is an important species in the marine ecosystem and plays a key role in maintaining the balance of the ocean.

53

The Mahi Mahi is a resilient species and has been able to adapt to changing conditions in its habitat.

The Mahi Mahi is a beautiful, fascinating fish that has been a part of Costa Rica's culture for thousands of years.

The Mahi Mahi is a schooling fish, which means that it travels in large groups that can number in the thousands.

The Mahi Mahi is a pelagic fish, meaning that it spends its life in the open ocean.

61

Conclusion

The Mahi Mahi is a remarkable fish that has been a part of Costa Rica's culture for thousands of years. It is an important food source for many people, an important species for recreational and commercial fisheries, and a top predator in its ecosystem. This book has explored 30 fun facts about the Mahi Mahi that will help you to learn more about this amazing fish and its environment.

Thank you for reading this book!

If you found this book helpful, I would be grateful if you would **post an honest review on Amazon** so this book can reach other supportive readers like you!

All you need to do is digitally flip to the back and leave your review. Or visit amazon.com/author/senseipauldavid click the correct book cover and click on the blue link next to the yellow stars that say, "customer reviews."

As always...

It's a great day to be alive!

Share Our FREE eBooks Now!

kidsonearth.life

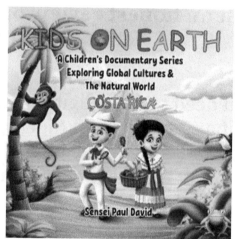

kidsonearth.world

Click Below for Another Book In Each Series

senseipublishing.com/KoE_SERIES

senseipublishing.com/KoE_Wildlife_SERIES

KoE En Español

senseipublishing.com/KoE_SERIES_SPANISH

www.senseipublishing.com

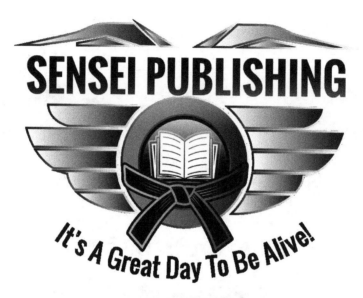

www.senseipublishing.com

@senseipublishing
#senseipublishing

Check out our **recommendations** for other books for adults &
kids plus other great resources by visiting
www.senseipublishing.com/resources/

Join Our Publishing Journey!

If you would like to receive FREE BOOKS and special offers, please visit www.senseipublishing.com and join our newsletter by entering your email address in the pop-up box

Follow Our Engaging Blog NOW!
senseipauldavid.ca

Get Our FREE Books Today!

Click & Share the Links Below

FREE Kids Books

lifeofbailey.senseipublishing.com
kidsonearth.senseipublishing.com

FREE Self-Development Book

senseiselfdevelopment.senseipublishing.com

FREE BONUS!!!
Experience Over 25 FREE Engaging Guided Meditations!

Prized Skills & Practices for Adults & Kids. Help Restore Deep Sleep, Lower Stress, Improve Posture, Navigate Uncertainty & More.

Download the Free Insight Timer App and click the link below:
http://insig.ht/sensei_paul

About Sensei Publishing

Sensei Publishing commits itself to helping people of all ages transform into better versions of themselves by providing high-quality and research-based self-development books with an emphasis on mental health and guided meditations. Sensei Publishing offers well-written e-books, audiobooks, paperbacks, and online courses that simplify complicated but practical topics in line with its mission to inspire people toward positive transformation.

It's a great day to be alive!

About the Author

I create simple & transformative eBooks & Guided Meditations for Adults & Children proven to help navigate uncertainty, solve niche problems & bring families closer together.

I'm a former finance project manager, private pilot, jiu-jitsu instructor, musician & former University of Toronto Fitness Trainer. I prefer a science-based approach to focus on these & other areas in my life to stay humble & hungry to evolve. I hope you enjoy my work and I'd love to hear your feedback.

- It's a great day to be alive!
Sensei Paul David

Scan & Follow/Like/Subscribe: Facebook, Instagram, YouTube: @senseipublishing

Scan using your phone/iPad camera for Social Media
Visit us at www.senseipublishing.com and sign up for our newsletter to learn more about our exciting books and to experience our FREE Guided Meditations for Kids & Adults.

Printed in the USA
CPSIA information can be obtained
at www.ICGtesting.com
LVHW082332120524
780094LV00032B/885

9 781778 484131